Ancient Palestine

FACETS

Ancient Palestine

A Historical Introduction

Gösta Ahlström

Fortress Press
Minneapolis

ANCIENT PALESTINE
A Historical Introduction

Cover and book design: Joseph Bonyata
Cover image: Vincent Soyez, 2002/nonstøck. Used by permission.

0-8006-3572-8

The paper used in this publication meets the minimum requirements of American National Standard for Information Sciences—Permanence of Paper for Printed Library Materials, ANSI Z329.48-1984.

Manufactured in the U.S.A.
06 05 04 03 02 1 2 3 4 5 6 7 8 9 10

Contents

This volume is a slightly revised version of the introduction to Gösta Ahlström's magisterial work, The History of Ancient Palestine *(1993). The full text of the introduction is presented here, and all the notes are included (though moved to the end). The changes we have made were incorporated for the sake of the general reader and to compensate for the separation of this essay from the 990-page volume. We have abbreviated a few of the very long footnotes, rephrased sentences that refer to the longer work, and added a few explanatory words and phrases for clarity.*

We want to take this opportunity to renew our thanks to Diana V. Edelman for the vast amount of editorial work she put into the original edition.

Introduction

History and Historiography

Thus I write, as the truth seems to be to me.
  —Hecataeus of Miletus[1]

This quotation from Hecataeus describes in a nutshell what history-writing looked like in the ancient world. The writer relied upon what was seen, heard, and understood—a "method" also used by Herodotus. However, the modern idea of history did not exist in ancient times, which presents the problem of finding the "history" of those times. That task will be more involved for us than for the ancients because of the accumulated source material that is available to the modern historian.

Four points have to be made here. We have to discover, if possible, not only (1) what happened, but also (2) how the events were understood by the ancient writers, (3) how these writers wanted it to have happened, that is, the purpose of the writing, and (4) the audience for whom they wrote.[2] Past time is forever gone, but we can construct part of it, depending upon the character of the available sources. Such a reconstruction is the task of historiography, an art that includes a presentation of sources, their interpretation, and, as a last resort, hypotheses that may solve some problems and in a logical way fill the gaps in the source material. History is thus not an exact science, because we do not know all the facts.[3]

Writing history—historiography—can be likened to an archaeologist's struggles to restore a beautiful Mycenaean jar. Even if less than 30 percent of it is available in both large and small pieces, much can be learned about its form and decoration. When the form and decorative pattern from these sherds are known or are made known through some of the indicative pieces, the form of the jar can be restored by filling in the gaps with modern clay. The beauty of the vessel can, however, never be fully restored. Logically, one can state what the decoration might have looked like, but one cannot predict whether this particular vessel was in complete harmony with known patterns or whether there were some deviations, (small) surprises, mistakes, or whether the jar was somewhat deformed. As the restorer of the jar can see the work completed but not see all the original details, so the historiographer can reconstruct the history of a certain period and its people, but cannot "see" all the events and changes of the lost society. The life of those who created history—in most cases, humans with their psychological problems—escapes us to a large extent.[4]

I need to mention certain aspects of historiography, most importantly, my understanding of the material on which this presentation will be based.[5] It goes without saying that the task of tracing the history of a region from prehistoric times through several millennia is an immense, albeit a fascinating, task. In the case of greater Palestine, it is an almost impossible task because of the different sources and sometimes the lack of reliable source material, no matter at what point in time one ends the investigation. Like most other historians, the Syro-Palestinian historian has two primary kinds of source material for a re-construction of the past: archaeological and literary. Information can also be de-rived from the geography and the climate of the region.

According to the usefulness of the mate-rial, distinctions must be made between ar-chaeological material and literary sources, as well as between primary and secondary sources. The secondary sources usually refer to textual material. A primary source is written at a time close to the event. It can be a report, a royal annal, a letter or an original story. Secondary material may be a copy of an original, an interpretive text, a rewriting, re-editing, distortion, falsifica-tion or the like.

In principle, archaeological material be-longs among the primary sources. It can often be used to corroborate and supple-ment textual material, but it can correct or even contradict it. In this way archaeologi-cal remains can give a more realistic un-derstanding of the societies they refer to, their trade and culture, and so forth.[6] How-ever, completely unknown or unmentioned facts may also be revealed by excavations, thus potentially causing established opinions to be revised.[7] Examples are the steel industry of the Baq'ah Valley in Transjordan from the Iron I period,[8] the Judahite temple at Arad in the Negev, and the finds from Kuntillet 'Ajrud referring to Yahweh and his Asherah, to mention only a few.[9]

No region has been "dug up" so completely that its history can be written based primarily on archaeological remains. It should also be remembered that Palestinian archaeology has been mainly "tell-minded." It is only during the last decades that surface surveys have been undertaken in any large measure, but thorough excavations of the countryside are the exception. However, archaeological source material can be seen to be "mute," and there is no method for exact dating. It does not tell the whole story by itself.[10] A stone is a stone, a wall is a wall. A grave, for instance, does not tell who dug it, and a mudbrick wall does not say anything *per se* about ethnicity. Yet other circumstances, such as the contents of the grave and the objects in the house, can give information about their respective societies.[11] The culture, habits, and political affairs of a people can be only partially reconstructed on the basis of archaeological remains. Information about the people's food supply and sometimes about diseases can be derived from excavated objects.[12] Even if objects and tools can to some extent indicate a community's sophistication, they will only provide a partial picture of the level of that sophistication. Thus, other information, such as textual material, is necessary for drawing conclusions that can be used for historiography. However, because mute sources and texts do not give all the necessary information, there will always be a need for a method that uses reasoning, hypotheses, logic, and imagination (in other words, the "clay" of the historian) in order to construct something from the available material and to fill in the gaps between the sources.

Among the mute sources can be included geographical changes. Some are permanent, some transient. Some are accidental; others are caused by people. Such changes include natural disasters like mudslides or volcanic eruptions, as well as purposeful alternations to the environment, such as the building of roads and canals, terracing, (de)forestation, the killing of game, and pollution.[13] All this is also evidence for history, and as such it needs to be part of the historiographic picture. There are, however, other random factors that are more problematic to come to grips with, such as a toothache making a ruler temporarily unable to make a sound judgment, or an epidemic reducing the population density in certain parts of a region, or terminating a military campaign, as might have been the case when the Assyrian king Sennacherib besieged Jerusalem in 701 B.C.E.

As mentioned, knowledge about geography and climate must be taken into consideration in historiography, to add to our understanding of problems like demography and changes in population density, and to answer the question of "why?" for certain events. Once someone has seen Buseira in Jordan, for instance, it is easy to understand why a city was built on that mountain plateau, which is surrounded by a natural "moat."[14] Mountains, valleys, rivers, seas, and deserts are of utmost importance for understanding settlement problems, and for learning about the population, its livelihood and its cultural achievements. The central hills of Palestine, being sparsely settled, were considered a place of refuge, as Josh 15:16 indicates. It should be noted that mountains "are as a rule a world apart from civilizations"—a statement that also can be used for large forested areas.[15] Trading posts along trade routes would have attracted certain groups of people as well as military powers, for whom trade and political domination were often identical. The same is the case with promontories and other places suitable for sea trade. Lucrative business opportunities at such places would have attracted people and thus made them open to both political and cultural growth. Examples of the latter are the Phoenician city states and the location of cities and harbors built during the Phoenician expansion to the West.[16]

Oral tradition can also play an important role for the historiographer who studies living societies. However, it cannot serve as a tool for dealing with dead cultures, in which it has to some extent become part of the literary source material.[17] Nevertheless, we may suspect that oral tradition was used to fill in the gaps in an ancient writer's presentation. In Greece, for instance, legends describing "events of the Bronze and

Dark Ages are highly suspect."[18] Because the Greek writers relied mainly on what they saw and on "reports from reliable witnesses," they would have had no material other than nonverifiable oral traditions when describing archaic periods.[19] Even though Herodotus is called the "father of history," his method was one based only on interviewing and listening, which was standard for that time. In certain instances his information might have been quite wrong. It is also uncertain to what extent he recounted stories that he may himself have doubted, just to entertain the "groundlings" in his audience.[20] Still, his importance lies in his being the first writer to collect a vast amount of information,[21] including geographical and historical facts, as well as stories and legends about the past from both reliable and unreliable persons.[22] All this is presented as a history of the world in his time; thus, his may be called the first "universal" history.

It seems indisputable that some written sources were based on oral traditions. The problem is how to establish what part of a text is built on a piece of oral tradition. It may turn out that what has been labeled oral tradition in some cases is nothing more than a legend or a saga, in other words, fiction.[23] An example would be the discussion between Jonathan and the conspirator David behind a bush (1 Sam 20:11-23). How can that "conversation" ever be established as an empirical fact?

The theory that most of the biblical material has been preserved by oral tradition over hundreds of years is untenable,[24] even though it is agreed that some literature must have had an oral prehistory before being fixed in its present written form.[25] Examples of such orally based literature would be cultic laws and psalms, which may have changed over time because of new situations or new needs.[26] In this connection, the role of memorization should also be noted, something that must have been part of priestly education and that would also have played an important role in prophetic circles. The words of a prophetic master were to be remembered, because they were divine words.[27]

A "source" thus functions as information that can be viewed as an answer to historical questions we pose. Sources are always limited in time and space. As for literary material, we are always faced with the problem of reliability. We always have to ask, With what kind of material are we dealing? Who wrote it? For whom was it written, and for what purpose? Can the text be trusted? What are its biases? Does it pretend to relate a divine promise, or is it written for a special purpose, as are, for instance, a law code, a sales contract, a treaty text, a letter, a genealogy, a king-list, a chronicle, an apology, or a piece glorifying a person, a myth, a story about a folk-hero? Are we dealing with a form of political-religious advocacy or doctrines? with an etiology? with telescoping or a distortion of events? or nothing other than fiction written as a fairytale? Is a particular text built upon another source and therefore, whether intentionally or not, altering it?

In addition, a text often includes literary patterns and "embroideries" that can make its reliability suspect—perhaps it is overemphasizing one aspect and neglecting another. Such can be the case with religious and political literary products. Political literature is common among ancient Near Eastern historical texts, which also use mythological[28] categories for describing unknown periods or the wonders and disasters of the world.[29] For instance, the beginning of history may start with the creation of the cosmos, which is understood as being the result of a divine action. Prehistoric time with its unknown events is often described in mythical categories in order to produce a link between the unknown and the known. Examples of such "mythological historiography" are the Babylonian cosmology with Marduk's battle against the chaos monster Tiamat, the concept of *tatenen,* "the primeval hill," which in ancient Egypt was thought of as rising out of the waters at the beginning of time.[30] The creation narratives in Genesis 1–11 are part of the same urge to explain how the cosmos once upon a time came into being and how life developed because of the divine will.[31] The Exodus legend with its motif of a people saved through the splitting of a sea also belongs to the same category of mythological fictions.[32] The same motif has been used in connection with the crossing of the Jordan river and the entry into Canaan (Josh 3:7–5:1). The entry is depicted as having been accomplished through a divine wonder.[33]

That concept is part of the late settlement theology.

This raises the question of what kind of "history" is expected in the stories about the Exodus and the wanderings in the wilderness, and its sequel, the "conquest" of Canaan. This text cycle, composed for religious purposes, is an attempt to explain how the people of Yahweh were created. It is also a kind of history; it is religious historiography, the goal of which is not to present empirical facts. Religion can create whatever "history" it wants or needs. The modern historian is here faced with two problems, and both are legitimate research objects: the actual history of the peoples/nations, and the history of their self-understanding and religion. In this volume I will be concerned with the former; thus, the religious historiography of the Exodus and the wanderings in the wilderness and the resultant ideology of an invasion and a conquest of Canaan will not solve any problems in the history of Palestine.[34] These texts deal with a certain people's self-understanding and not primarily with empirical history.[35] They are part of a religiously directed historiography.[36] Because there are no other literary sources for this period, the archaeology of Palestine will have to become the main source for historiography, and it shows a picture quite different from the religiously motivated writings.[37]

The language of religion is mythological in character, but this language was part of historiographical thinking in the ancient Near East.[38] Any event could be described as an act of the divine, which means that the description could be mythological or ideological, rather than factual, and that its details may therefore not be verifiable. This is common in Egyptian royal inscriptions, for example. The battle at Qadesh between the Hittites and the Egyptians may serve as a specific example. It almost ended in disaster for the Egyptian army, but Ramses II (1279–1212 B.C.E.) describes it as a victory for himself and his "father Amons," the main god of Thebes.[39] The "god-king" cannot be a loser. Sometimes a story takes on the character of being unnatural, as for instance, the splitting of the "Red Sea" in Exodus, or the drowning of all the Canaanites in Judges 5, in which only the commander Sisera managed to escape when the others drowned. (Did he run on water?) In this context the sea motif is a literary pattern.

Another example of how mythology could be used in expressing both the royal ideology and its connection with creation is found in Psalm 89. The election of David and his enthronement is presented in the liturgical activity as taking place after Yahweh had defeated the chaos powers and then made his creation.[40] Modern standards of historicity were not part of the ancient world's intellectual life.

The examples mentioned above can show the applicability of J. Huizinga's observation that "every civilization creates its own form of history."[41] This kind of history can be labeled "imaginary history," because it is an expression of a people's self-understanding and is in principle not necessarily based on any empirical events. Only when a people has had a certain amount of time to organize itself can it begin to consider the question of common origin.[42] Not enough is known about all the peoples living in the ancient Near East to accept Huizinga's statement as expressing a rule without exception. For instance, nothing is known about the beginning of a concept of history and its development among the Moabites, the Ammonites, Edomites, or Aramaeans, to mention only a few. It can only be assumed that they may have had concepts somewhat similar to those common in the Near East of their time. Migrations, trade connections, political vassalage, deportations, intermarriages, and so forth, might have contributed to a common ideological "language" among the Semitic peoples. Myths could "travel." The importance of scribal schools has also to be considered when studying the spread of legends, myths, and folktales.

Certain Babylonian legends and myths could have become known to Judahites for the first time after they had been deported to Babylonia. Some historical and geographical knowledge about Mesopotamia may have first become known to the people of Judah during the Exile. For instance, the stories about Nimrod (Gen 10:8) and the Tower of Babel (Gen 11:1-9) were most probably composed after the Judahites had been exiled and had become familiar with Babylonian phenomena. They would most probably not have been intelligible before the Exile.

The phrase "Ur of the Chaldeans" (Gen 11:31; 15:7; and Neh 9:7) is an anachronism before the ninth century B.C.E.[43] The Sumerian city of Ur declined in the second millennium but saw a revival under Babylonia's last king, Nebuna'id, in the sixth century B.C.E.[44] Did some of the exiled people learn about this city after they had been taken to Babylonia? If so, that could lead to the conclusion that the whole Abraham story is not a piece of history but rather is a literary product aimed at a religious and political situation of a much later time than its supposed Bronze Age setting.[45]

All these aspects have to be considered by anyone who presents a historiographic picture of the peoples of the ancient Near East. In addition, an awareness of the scholarly interpretation of the material is necessary—an interpretation that often might be influenced by cultural trends or the modern historiographer's background within such a trend (Romanticism, Positivism, Idealism, Marxism, cyclical theories, confessional background and so on), which is part of this historiographer's worldview.

For most periods of the history of Palestine the archaeological remains are of the utmost importance.[46] Nothing could be written about certain periods if these remains did not exist or were unknown. This is true not only for the preliterary periods, but also for periods that are represented by textual material, as well as periods in which writing was practiced, but from which no textual records have survived. Times that are completely unchronicled by local written records are, for example, the Early Bronze Age and the Iron I Age. There are no texts from the Egyptian or Mesopotamian kingdoms that describe life and the political circumstances in Palestine and Transjordan during the latter period. Egyptian sources talk about the invasion of the so-called Sea Peoples and their march through Palestine. The result of their unsuccessful invasion of Egypt is now known from the archaeology of the settlements of the Philistines on the coast. One Egyptian papyrus, containing the story of Wenamun's journey to Byblos, mentions that the Tjeker people had settled at Dor south of Carmel.[47] In general, it can be said that the Near Eastern powers during this period were at a "low ebb." The unstable political situation in the Levant did not encourage or require any great scribal activity in Akkadian, as had been the case during the Bronze Age. Interestingly, however, the Late Bronze II and Iron Ages were times when alphabetic writing developed and when the old Akkadian syllabic cuneiform was replaced in many places by more practical styles of writing, such as the Phoenician alphabet. Groups of people moving to the very sparsely settled hill country of Palestine from different areas were perhaps not those who were trained in the art of writing. Therefore, it cannot be assumed that they wrote anything down about their past history. They were refugees, pioneers, or resettled nomads not connected with each other by any ethnic or political bonds. Their problem was to establish themselves and their villages and to make life possible economically. Writing a "history" about how they arrived at this or that place could not yet have become part of their life. They had no need for that yet. This simply means that, for the period usually labeled Iron Age I, which includes the time of the so-called Judges, there are no extrabiblical literary

sources for the history of this region beyond the information about the so-called
Sea Peoples.

A most difficult problem facing a modern historian is the treatment of that part of
the history of Palestine, which includes the
peoples of Israel and Judah. The history
that can be detected concerning these peoples is fragmented, despite the wealth of literary material, or rather, because of it. As
mentioned above, the biblical writers had a
completely different goal than that of the
modern historian; the problem, therefore, is
to discover what real events if any can be
found in these writings. From this it follows
that the historiography of certain periods
for which there are no other sources available than those of the biblical writers will
rest on shaky ground because of the sub-
jective presentation and religious perspective (*Tendenz*) of the material.

Some attention should be given here to
the problem of the prehistory of Israel and
Judah, especially since A. Malamat has
voiced the opinion that such a concept as
"the prehistory of Israel" should be
avoided. It would refer to a time when no
Israel existed. He prefers instead the term

protohistory. Malamat sees the dividing line between "protohistory" and actual history as being the period when "the migratory movements of the Israelites had effectively come to an end," that is, when the tribes had "consolidated what were to be their hereditary holdings."[48] Malamat's stance merely transforms the biblical historiographic pattern into an empirical event. Archaeology does not support such a reconstruction. An evolution from tribe to nation is a questionable hypothesis.[49] Some tribal names might originally have been territorial names, which would mean that the "tribe" is a late development.[50] It seems to me, therefore, that the term *prehistory* is accurate as long as the existence of any sociopolitical organization called Israel cannot be established. Malamat acknowledges that the "Bible does not present authentic documents contemporary to events described"; thus, his theory about a "protohistory" is weakened. He tries to see the Merneptah stele, which mentions the name Israel, as a contemporary source for a "pan-Israelite league of twelve tribes, or a more limited group."[51] This is no more than speculation, because the Merneptah stele does not clarify anything about the social organization of the people Israel that it mentions as being in Palestine. Malamat's "protohistory" looks very much like a rewriting of the biblical narratives. As a matter of fact, a "protohistory" of Israel and Judah would include Adam and Eve, which can be concluded from the genealogies in Genesis 5 and 10; thus, there is no need to write any such history. The Hebrew Bible has already done it.[52]

It should be emphasized that in dealing with any society in Palestine the problem is that a mere presentation of facts, as they are understood, is not historiography, because it does not include all the facts. It is therefore no more than an incomplete catalogue. From the available facts certain deductions can be made and the picture thereby filled out. Reasons have to be found, if possible, for the events within a community or nation, and other circumstances that would have affected public or private life. When dealing with the ancient Near East, and with Palestine in particular, however, it is very seldom that a picture can be drawn of the common people's life. Almost nothing is known about how the role of religion affected the individual, about military service, sales contacts, freedom, divorce, adoption, serfdom, or to whom one was sold into slavery.[53] Archaeological material can provide some insight into the life of a household or of a village, a city or a fortress, but the individual disappears from the record. This is to be expected, because the common person did not write down an account of events. Therefore, there always will be blank spots in the historical picture.

Some periods are more or less difficult to deal with because of the paucity of both textual and archaeological material. For parts of Palestine such a period is the Late Bronze Age. For instance, there are many archaeological remains in the valleys and on the coast, but because the LB Age was a time of very few settlements in the central hills, the archaeological picture will be very spotty.[54] However, the tablets from Tell el-Amarna contain the correspondence between the Pharaoh and his Syro-Palestinian vassals during the fourteenth century B.C.E. The tablets, written in Akkadian, talk about a number of city states in the lowlands and the valleys, but only about a very few in the central hills, namely Shechem and Jerusalem, and Pehel (Pella) in the foothills of Jordan close to the Jordan Valley. How much history do these texts relate? A literary analysis shows a formulaic language with common ideas, such as defense for a city-king's actions and his demands on the Pharaoh to protect and help him with his problems with neighboring city-states, robbers, and so on. The problem with these letters is not "to ascertain if a narrated event is 'true', but why it has been stated in that particular way and not in another."[55] In other words, what kinds of motives were there for the letters to be written? There is no corroborative material that can be used, nor is there any information about the chain of events or the context that led to the writing beside what the letters mention.[56] Thus, a history cannot really be written from these texts, but the letters are useful for filling in some gaps in the political and demographic picture of this period.

A period completely unknown in Near Eastern texts except from the Hebrew Bible is that of the so-called united monarchy. No kingdom called Israel or Judah, much less an Israelite empire, is anywhere attested in the records of the non-Palestinian countries.[57] This may be due to the fact that the Egyptian and Assyrian powers were at a low ebb in this period; thus they had no interaction with any kingdom in Palestine. A presentation of the history of this period, as of any other period in the history of Palestine that lacks external evidence, will therefore be tentative. This is not to deny that there is any reliable information in the biblical texts, but, without the corroboration of external source material, the picture that can be presented from an examination of Judges, Samuel, and 1 Kings—the texts that are available—will be no more than a discussion of what could have been possible. However, when this is supplemented with the archaeological remains, the plausibility of a kingdom in the hills has to be acknowledged. This period shows an intensification of building activities, not only of small farmsteads and villages, but also of monumental buildings such as fortresses, of cities with a certain type of fortification and city gates, and of government building projects, such as store cities. The conclusion to be drawn from all this is that such activities were the result of a governmental policy.

As an example of how some history can be extracted from certain propagandistic textual material, the narratives about King Saul and some of his deeds may be mentioned. The main argument for the existence of Saul and his kingdom is the fact that the biblical writers so strongly and so often emphasize that David, the usurper, was the "chosen one." The fact that Saul is said to have fallen from divine grace as ruler shows the writer's problem with an "ideologically" disturbing personality. If Saul had been an insignificant or nonexistent person, this emphasis would not have been necessary. If Saul did not have to be accounted for, the writers would rather have done as in Egypt; erased the memory of an "unwanted" or "evil" king. Obviously Saul was of such a stature that he could not be gotten around or ignored. Thus, for instance, the laconic information in 1 Sam 14:47 about Saul having battled Moab, Ammon, Edom, Beth-Rehob, and the Aramaean king of Zobah, as well as the Philistines, may be true.

Here arises the difficult question about the reliability of the biblical texts as source material and about how they relate to what history really looked like. This leads to the problem of methodology. Because of the diversity of the source material (textual, archaeological, geographical, and so on) there is no one method that can be used to deal with the different sources. For instance, literary patterns, myths, and sagas do not relate history; thus any method used for such texts cannot reveal the course of historical events, because the texts were not written for such a purpose. As to the historical books of the Bible, including the historical information in the prophetical books, the methods of literary criticism, form criticism and source criticism, each of which supplements the others, as well as redaction criticism, may be used in some instances. However, these are methods that are used to clarify the history of a *text* and its *composition;*[58] this does not *ipso facto* mean that through such methods we reach the historical event.[59]

For instance, a literary analysis of Judges 3–9 shows a composition made up of smaller units, that is, stories about chieftains, tribes, clans, and so on in the so-called premonarchic period of Israel.[60] The first step of an analysis would be to see in what literary context this complex has been placed. It turns out to be part of a literary pattern that has decided the place of the smaller units. This is the ancient Near Eastern historiographic pattern of change between "good" and "evil." A good time is followed by an evil time, fortune is followed by misfortune, light is followed by darkness.[61] The next step would be to identify the smaller units and the kind of literary categories to which they belong: the stories about Othniel, Ehud, Shamgar, Deborah and Barak, Gideon, Jerubbaal, and Abimelech. These persons represent in the pattern the "good" leaders of "all Israel" (as the historiographic phrase has it), except for Abimelech. The other leaders have all followed an "evil" period. The altar tradition connected with Gideon (Judg 6:11-17) may reflect a special source or tradition referring to an event that contributed to Gideon's fame. As the next step, can it now be determined from what sources these writings derived? The answer will be no. It simply is not known whether these stories were part of certain older writing(s) available to the narrator or whether they were compositions inspired by certain oral traditions, fictitious or not. Neither form nor redaction criticism can uncover what the exact history looked like in these cases, because no material exists that shows the text in an earlier stage.[62]

The story about the Yeminite Ehud freeing the "Israelites" from Moabite oppression (Judg 3:12-30) can be used as an example of how "knowledge" about a certain person has been utilized by the narrator.[63] First of all, it should be noted that this story is quite different from the preceding one about Othniel, which contains but a few statements. The Ehud narrative is in contrast a humorous and ironical folkloristic hero-story, which may have existed first in an oral tradition, which has been used by the D historian, who included Ehud among the "saviors" of the people of Yahweh.[64] There was probably a source, a tradition, about Ehud that the writer made into a well-structured composition contrasting the man of "glory," Ehud, with the fat king of Moab, the oppressor Eglon.[65]

The narrative has three scenes with actions
and speeches (vv. 19, 20-23, 24-25), and it
ends with the act of Ehud and his men vic-
toriously battling the Moabites (vv. 26-30).
Certain phrases recur, such as "the p^esîlîm,
'gods,' at Gilgal" (vv. 19 and 26). The text
also includes a pun on the word yāmîn,
"south," or "right side."[66] Like all the other
"judges," Ehud has been seen as a leader
over "all Israel." He supposedly had been
chosen to pay the tribute to Moab's king,
Eglon, who was said to have enslaved the
Israelites for eighteen years (vv. 12-14).
Having killed the king of Moab, Ehud fled
and came to "Israel" and blew trumpets in
Mt. Ephraim so the "Israelites" joined him
and cut off Moab from access to the fords
of the Jordan (vv. 26-30).[67] The important
literary points in the text are the descrip-
tions of Ehud and Eglon, and how Ehud
killed the king who represents the evil
power. Ehud had to use his left hand because the right one was paralyzed, and
through treachery he killed the Moabite
king.[68] The latter is described as being very
fat. His name is an ironical pun on the Hebrew 'ēgel ("calf"); in other words, Eglon is

pictured as a fat young bull, an ideal animal for the holocaust sacrifice. The rest of the "details" are embroidery.[69]

As a result of a closer look at the text the history disappears. Literary-critical observations do not contribute any historicity to the related events. The narrative is probably a hero story about a local chieftain, whom we cannot exactly place in time, but who in the Bible has been assigned to the pre-monarchic period. It should also be noted that the only Moabite kingdom known from the period before King Saul is the one that is represented by the Balu'a stela from c. 1200 B.C.E., from the area just south of Wadi Mujib (c. 24 km north of Kerak). What political unit the king of the stela represents is not known. He could have been a nomadic chieftain, to judge from his clothing.[70] It is improbable that any Moabite kingdom in the period before Saul could have reached as far north as the territories of the Jordan river, especially if the Ammonites were expanding westward. The historicity of Eglon and Ehud is not enhanced by any textual, form or redaction criticism. The result of an analysis of the text is that Ehud and Eglon can only be described as the two main characters in a literary drama.[71] The same conclusion can be drawn concerning the narratives about the other "judges."[72]

From the above it is evident that even if the form of a text can be outlined and the different units separated, establishing some repeated phraseology and detecting some intrusions, all that will result is a history of the text and not the certification of actual events. All these different elements have been woven together by the narrator in order to give a total picture in which some events of the past can be seen to have been part of the people's history. Some other events may have been adapted according to the writer's intentions, others may be fictitious, and some may not have been considered at all.

The above is true in most cases. However, literary analysis, as well as redaction criticism, may now and then help to establish the probability of an event. For instance, Judges 4 and 5 recount the same battle between a Canaanite coalition and certain Israelites, according to the writers. This is not the place to give a complete literary analysis of these texts. But because

Judges 4 is a narrative while Judges 5 is a poem in archaic style that contains other topics than those in Judges 4, the compositions may be seen to stem from different hands. Judges 5 is a victory hymn composed of various motifs, such as a theophany (vv. 4-5) and reminiscences of past, glorious times including the time of Shamgar, Jael, and Deborah (vv. 6-7).[73] In common with other Near Eastern victory hymns, the "Song of Deborah," as it has been called, expresses the idea that deities effect a miraculous wonder for their own people. The goal of the theophany is to lead up to the "historical" victory.[74]

Judges 4 and 5 have been redacted in a sequence, but the content is different, even if they both deal with the same leaders and their forces. What they have in common is that both texts mention Zebulon and Naphtali as fighting the enemies. This could be redactional, but because Judges 4 does not state that any other group of people joined Zebulon and Naphtali, these two "tribes" must be original in Judges 4. The poem adds some other "tribes" that do not, however, participate in the battle. Even though no corroborating nonbiblical texts are available, from a methodological point of view we must take into consideration what is known about the political situation in Syria-Palestine in the so-called premonarchic period. Thus, the question must be asked: Can the battle between the "Canaanites" under Sisera and the "Israelites" under Barak (with the prophetic support of Deborah) really have occurred during the period Late Bronze II–Iron I Ages? Realizing that Egypt dominated Palestine into the mid-twelfth century B.C.E., followed by the power of the Philistines, a battle between two large coalitions in the strategically important Jezreel plain is out of the question. Without going into all the literary problems of Judges 5 (which could occupy a whole book), I can conclude that the battle was a local event that was utilized by the composer of the poem at a later time and thus has been given an "all-Israelite" case. From that point of view, Judges 5 is less historical than Judges 4. However, this does not say anything for certain about the date of the two compositions.

The Near Eastern literary phenomenon of a repeated change between an ideal and or-

derly period to an evil period of chaos is a
device often occurring in so-called
prophetic texts using such motifs as light
and darkness, fortune and misfortune,
blessing and curse.[75] This literary device is
also heavily used by biblical narrators and
prophets. The so-called deuteronomic history work (i.e. the books of Deuteronomy,
Joshua, Judges, Samuel and Kings) has
structured its historiography according to
this kind of pattern.[76] For instance, the period of the so-called Judges (excluding the
appended chapters 17–21) is presented as
an era during which "the people of Israel"
often abandoned the "right" religion of
Yahweh and were therefore oppressed by
enemies until Yahweh heard their laments
and "raised up a judge" to lead them. When
he died the people again abandoned Yahweh, and after a time of oppression Yahweh
had to give the people another "judge." This
"light and dark periods" scheme also occurs
as the basis for the evaluation of the kings
of Judah.[77] Such a literary pattern cannot
be used for a reconstruction of history.[78]

A parallel to this literary pattern of
change between "good" and "evil" rulers

can be found in Babylonian literature, in the so-called Weidner Chronicle, for instance. The Chronicle is a piece of religious propaganda, denouncing kings who did not care enough for Marduk and his temple in Babylon.[79] Corresponding to this phenomenon, Ahaz of Judah is presented as an unfaithful "Yahwist" who therefore is "evil," but his son Hezekiah is seen as an ideal king. Hezekiah's son Manasseh, as well as Manasseh's successor, Amon (who did not really count because he was murdered after two years), were "evil." Josiah is then hailed as being a king as "good" as Hezekiah and David. This is an example of the one-sidedness of biblical historiography and of how this "historiography" follows an ideological pattern. It is not really concerned with facts. Historically, King Hezekiah led his nation of Judah to the brink of disaster, but in the eyes of the biblical narrator he scored the highest points as a "righteous" king because he was a good "disciple" who followed the advice of the prophet Isaiah. For the biblical writer, nothing was more important than to follow the divine words that were expressed by the divine law or through a prophet who was acceptable to and in harmony with the writer's ideology.

An example of this ideology is expressed by the demand that the king obey the law, *torah* (Deut 17:18-20). Among other things this text states that the king must write a copy of the *torah* "at the dictation of the Levitical priests," and that he must read it every day as long as he lives. What king would have had the time to study the *torah* every day? Administratively this is quite impossible. This text is a clear indication that the composition of the Bible is late and that this statute (which is reminiscent of the rabbinic ideal) was written when no king was on the Davidic throne any longer. The biblical writer has here presented his ideal.

The basis for this kind of literature is religious zeal, which can use literary patterns, make adaptions, corrections, and sometimes fictional writings, as well as include exact events and exclude others, when it suits the authors' purpose. It could be asked, for instance, why the Judahite temple at Arad in the Negev is never mentioned in the Bible, or why the phenomenon of Yahweh having had a consort, Asherah, has been suppressed. She, too, was worshiped in the Solomonic temple, as was Baal. Why did King Manasseh of Judah become the scapegoat for the disasters of Judah that led up to the Exile? This king maintained peace during his 55-year reign and restored the official Judahite religion in the cities that were returned to Judah from Philistine administration. Manasseh restored the orthodox religion of Judah in these cities, which for some time after Hezekiah's reign must have had Philistine officials and priests or Philistine deities in charge of daily life.[80] Because all this did not suit the ideology of the biblical writers, who had a special purpose in mind when writing, Manasseh became a literary scapegoat.

The above indicates something about the principles guiding the writers of the Hebrew Bible. The material is specially selected and represents the concepts of a group that advocated a certain line of action and a certain way of thinking about the history of the people of Israel and Judah and their "untrustworthy" neighbors. It is doubtful that the group propagating deuteronomistic ideas represented the official ideology of pre-exilic society. The prophetical concepts by which the writers seem to have been influenced were not the official line of thinking in the kingdoms of Israel and Judah, as can be seen from the prophetical polemics against the official religions of these two states. It should also be noted that there was only a small group of prophets that was accepted by this group of tradents, namely those whose utterances could be used or were in line with the theological conceptualization of history of the writers and/or the collectors of the material.

The above shows that my approach has been to gather not only literary information, but also to a large extent archaeological material, in order to get as close as possible to the actual events. The approach also includes critical assessment of the biblical material against the political and cultural situation that can be learned from extrabiblical sources.

Empirical history and the religious, biblical concept of history have usually been mixed in scholarly presentations of the origin of Israel. The religious historiography does not *per se* need to build upon any reality, because religion makes its own reality, as mentioned above. Thus, there is

a special purpose for this kind of writing.
The biblical texts dealing with the origin
of Israel in Palestine belong to this kind of
historiography, because they proclaim that
behind the creation of the people Israel is
the divine will. Therefore they do not provide any basic information about the
emergence of the people or nation Israel.[81]
As to the date, the texts locating Israelites
in the eastern Nile delta cannot be earlier
than the seventh century, when the Saitic
26th Dynasty was in power and when the
Wadi Tumilat, part of the biblical land of
Goshen, began to be heavily settled.[82] It
can therefore be maintained that the demographic and thus also the cultural situation in the Nile delta known to the
narrator of the "sojourn in Egypt" has
been adapted to his historiography.

When the inscriptional material from the
Late Bronze period is considered, it is quite
clear that the biblical writers knew nothing
about events in Palestine before the tenth
century B.C.E. There are no traces of the so-
called Amarna period (fourteenth century
B.C.E.) known from the correspondence between the Pharaoh and the Syro-Palestinian
kinglets. There is no recollection whatso-

ever of the Egyptian dominion over Syria-Palestine during the Late Bronze period. The biblical writers do not know about the many Egyptian military campaigns through Palestine, which often resulted in destroyed cities and the taking of cattle and prisoners of war to Egypt. "There are, both in Exodus and in Judges, no heroic Pharaohs striding like *colossoi* across the map of the Near East, no marching armies of conquerors," no tribute paying city states, "no cities established in Pharaoh's name."[83] The events recorded in Pharaoh Merneptah's victory stele, mentioning that he had taken Ashkelon, Gezer, and Yeno'am and eradicated the people Israel from the earth,[84] are completely unknown, as is the march of the Sea Peoples through Palestine down to Egypt, which resulted in the settlement of Philistines and Tjeker people on the coast south of Carmel. The first Egyptian Pharaoh mentioned by name in the Bible is Shoshenq (biblical Shishak) of the 22nd Dynasty, to whom Jeroboam was to have fled after opposing Solomon (1 Kgs 11:40). This Pharaoh is also the first one that the biblical narrator credits with a march through Palestine, five years after Solomon's death

(1 Kgs 14:25-27a; 1 Chron 12:1-12). The biblical information about this campaign is corroborated in Shoshenq's inscription on a pylon of Amun's temple at Karnak (Thebes). The Egyptian account, on the other hand, mentions neither Israel, nor Judah nor Jerusalem, thus the biblical text about this Pharaoh's campaign can be seen to supplement the Egyptian information.[85] It can be concluded, however, that the biblical historiography dealing with the periods before Shoshenq primarily presents an imaginary history that builds on a few memories of a past time, such as the existence of Saul's kingdom.[86]

The documentary hypothesis for the Pentateuch developed by K. H. Graf and J. Wellhausen (with its sources J, E, P, and D) is of no real use for writing the early history of Israel and Judah, which Wellhausen himself understood.[87] No one has been able to demonstrate the independent existence of any of these literary complexes (besides D, which is mainly the book of Deuteronomy).[88] A priestly code, cut in pieces and affixed between several different stories with whatever kind of ideological glue, never existed as an independent literary source. It is quite another thing to state that there are many sacral laws in the Hebrew Bible occurring in different literary compositions. As in all societies, law-giving is an ongoing process. It is thus natural that we find laws in the Hebrew Bible that reflect both a pre-exilic and a postexilic condition.[89]

In this connection, the question of who the writers in the ancient Near East usually were could be asked. The main part of the literature of these Near Eastern societies including those of Palestine was most probably written by professionals, such as learned scribes and savants, who could be found in the government, the court, schools, temples and wisdom circles, or else by the nonprofessional elite.[90] There were, for instance, business transactions that also required some trained scribes. Most scribes were writing for a special audience or for a special purpose.[91] In a time when not everybody could read or write, the school became "an ideological molder of minds."[92] Scribes therefore became important persons not only representing the accumulated wisdom of a society, but also having the ability to advance to important positions in the government, as was the case with the scribe Setau, who became a viceroy under Ramses II.[93]

The question of how and when historiography in the ancient Near East began merits a book of its own. Royal inscriptions from Anatolia, Mesopotamia, and Egypt may represent the beginning of ancient Near Eastern historiographic activity. Egyptian and Sumerian inscriptions are the oldest examples. Annals occur in Hatti c. 300 years before the earliest Assyrian ones (from about the thirteenth century B.C.E.).[94] Most royal inscriptions represent the recording and glorification of royal deeds, but no real concept of historiography. Egyptian inscriptions and reliefs, for instance, often report certain happenings and conflicts with neighboring peoples, but this is mostly done in order to show how the might of Egypt prevailed. There is no continuous history. Reports about the kings and their deeds, such as campaigns to Syrian-Palestine, display the same style and the same kind of phraseology and literary patterns. They always praise the "divine" king. This indicates that the students in the scribal schools were trained in "the use of common patterns, with little change throughout the ages.[95] Thus the Egyptian material is not "much concerned with historical data on a war past the point of the enemy's defeat.[96] In other words, many of the details are literary stereotypes.

Concerning Babylonia, the "scribes simply wished to record what had happened in and around their land." This could be called history "written for history's sake." Its character is "parochial."[97] There is no national historiography in Babylonia before the neo-Babylonian empire emerged on the stage of history. In Assyria, collections of cuneiform tablets in libraries, such as that of Ashurbanipal, may have inspired research into the past, and the Babylonian Chronicles series could be seen as a result of such research.[98]

If national historiography first started in Babylonia in the eighth century B.C.E., might not Hebrew historiography be later, considering that Israel and Judah were relatively young nations? I do not want to deny the possibility that some biblical history-writing occurred earlier. Some annalistic writings may have been authored in the courts of Saul, Eshbaal, David, and Solomon. A decision on this matter must

be based on what could have been proba-
ble in such young nations that were located in the hills outside the mainstream of
cultural and material exchange, and that
developed relatively late as political units.
It must have taken a few hundred years of
common life before these small nations
could have developed some general views
about their history, especially if it is remembered that the different groups of
people that settled in the hills would have
needed a certain amount of time to meld
together and feel or develop a nationality,
not to say an ethnicity.[99] It is difficult,
therefore, to accept the hypothesis that a
historiographer, the so-called Yahwist
(J),[100] could have written a prehistory of
the people of Yahweh during the period of
the early monarchy,[101] when the people of
Judah[102] and Israel had not yet melded together—which they never really did in any
case. It seems that they might have been
"forced" into a union under David and
Solomon, because after Solomon's death
they fought each other until the period of
the Omrides in Israel.[103]

The most likely type of "historiography"
to have been written during the period of

the early monarchy would have been an apologetic for David's usurpation of the throne. The deuteronomistic emphasis on David as the chosen one points in this direction. The information that, after Sheba's uprising against David, the people of Israel was treated as a suppressed people, as a vassal nation, does not show that any intimate bond connected these two groups of people. Therefore, the composition of any historiography before Sheba's rebellion can be question. With the textual material available, it is impossible to answer that questioned. Another time when the peoples of Israel and Judah were closely connected was during the time of the Omrides, when there were intermarriages between the two royal houses and a common foreign policy. Such a period could have inspired the beginning of a "common" historiography.

However, the Bible's reconstruction of the "people" of Israel as twelve tribes with their origin in the prehistoric period raises the suspicion that this is part of a politically useful literary attempt to give Israel and Judah a common origin. After the fall of Israel in 722/721 B.C.E., the southern kingdom Judah could see itself as the remnant of the people of Yahweh.[104] This attitude, which is to be found among some prophets, may have inspired the biblical writers in their reconstruction of the "divinely guided" history.

The presentation of the history and life of any society in the ancient Near East can only be a torso because of the paucity of information. In addition, it must be realized that much of what was written down was carefully selected by the writer in order to promote his viewpoint.[105] The writing may have referred to a king's "glorious" campaigns, or his rationale for usurping the throne; it may have reflected the concepts of a religious reformer or propagandist; or it could have recounted folktales about past times and their heroes, the memory of which was quite blurred or not at all known. In such matters the biblical narrators were not really concerned about historical truth.[106] Their goal was not that of a modern historian—the ideal of "objectivity" had not yet been invented. In writing their "historiography" they maintained that their view of the past corresponded to Yahweh's view. Sometimes their historical novels are no more than that: novels. The stories about the so-called premonarchic period starting with creation are not history. They are literary creations.[107] Just as, for instance, Shakespeare wrote about Richard III, a biblical writer could compose a story about Abraham's journeys from Mesopotamia to Egypt or a story about Joseph and his brothers in Egypt. In these cases they have created some interesting pieces of literature, but not necessarily history. This is pure literature serving the purpose of religious ideology, and, in the case of the Abraham and Joseph stories, literature being used as part of a particular historiographic reconstruction.

In this connection it should be noted that "new moral and political ideas are often presented in the guise of traditional literature or ascribed to revered personages of the distant past."[108] Literature ascribed to such persons will naturally cause problems for the modern historiographer.

Most important for a history of the greater Palestinian area during the pre-Hellenistic period is the inscriptional material from neighboring countries, especially from Egypt, Anatolia, Assyria, and Babylonia. The reader may find that on occasion in *The History of Ancient Palestine* I relied more on Assyrian and Babylonian inscriptions than on Hebrew Bible texts relating to the same period. This stems from the fact that even if there are exaggerations and propagandistic tendencies in the nonbiblical material as well, the royal inscriptions of Mesopotamia have been engraved by royal scribes, who were employed by the kings in order to report and magnify the importance of their imperial campaigns and other events, such as building activities. These scribes did not invent such happenings as the capture of foreign cities, the flaying of a king, the devastation or incorporation of enemy territories, the deportation of thousands of people together with their gods, treasures, and cattle and so on.[109] It is noteworthy that there is no criticism of Akkadian kings in the Akkadian royal inscriptions. That would have been fatal for the scribe.

The Hebrew Bible "historiographers" were not, however, royal scribes. Even if they had some knowledge about material from the monarchic period, such as the "Book of Deeds of Solomon" (1 Kgs 11:41)[110] and the "Book of the Chronicles of the Kings of Israel/Judah" (1 Kgs 14:19,

29),[111] they probably used it freely. The references to these "books" are of a nature such that nothing is known about their contents. What is mentioned of Solomon's deeds in 1 Kings is not presented in chronological order and is, therefore, not strictly based on any annals or chronicles to which the narrator had access.[112] Most of the historiographic writings of the Hebrew Bible emerged during the time when no Israelite or Judahite king was in power, so the writers could not be punished or censored for the antiroyal attitude they often displayed. A Judahite writer, on the other hand, denouncing an Israelite king after Jehu's coup d'état in 841 B.C.E., would have been appreciated by the Jerusalemite court.

One thing these scribes had in common was the idea that the gods directed world events. The will of the divine was behind earthly actions. For instance, wars were undertaken at the "command" of the deities of the land, whether Ishtar, Teshub, Marduk, Amun, Ashur, Yahweh, Ahura Mazda, or Chemosh, to name but a few.[113] The god's territory, "cosmos," that is, his nation, had to be expanded. Those who opposed him belonged to the powers of evil and had therefore to be annihilated.

The intention of *The History of Ancient Palestine* was not to write a theological history of Bible lands. There are already too many of these. My goal has been to try to write a history of ancient Palestine in the same way that the history of any other region and all of its people is normally written.[114] Theological evaluations are therefore not to be found in it.[115] The aim has been to look at events as a historiographer, not through the eyes of the biblical narrators who treated the neighboring peoples as a "disturbing" factor in the lives of Israel and Judah, God's (usually wayward) children. Because of the character of the source material, my task has been a fascinating one. At the same time it has been not only difficult, but sometimes very frustrating. This is in part due to the religious and propagandistic character of the Hebrew Bible; the Bible is not a textbook in history, and it was never intended to be one. Events were seen from a special point of view and those that were not in harmony with this ideological viewpoint may have been "adapted" or else not considered at all.

What is regarded as history can only emerge from the result of the historiographer's work. The task of establishing what happened in the past is the ideal, but it can be no more than an interpretation; the full truth is never going to be revealed.[116] In principle the full truth may be called "history," but from a scientific viewpoint only part of history can be revealed, as the crushed Mycenaean jar can only be partly restored. The available facts are the potsherds, but their history comes about in the reconstruction.

Periodization

A historical chronology of Palestine and Syria should start with the period from which the first human remains are known. That means that the earliest period, the Paleolithic Age (the Stone Age), could have begun as far back as 1,500,000 or 600,000 years ago, depending upon where the possibilities for human life were found. The earliest known human remains in Palestine are from 'Ubeidiya from the so-called Lower Paleolithic period (Lower and Middle Pleistocene pluvial periods).[117] The site is located in the central Jordan Valley about 23 km south of Lake Tiberias near modern Afikim.[118]

The Paleolithic time is usually divided into three subperiods and is followed by the Epipaleolithic period, which in the Levant is also divided into subperiods according to archaeological remains, such as tools and other artifacts. The following chronological chart (pp. 56–57) gives the approximate dates of the different periods dealt with in this book. It should be remembered that a period does not start simultaneously in the different geographical areas. Thus, for instance, Egyptian chronology of the Nile delta in the Middle Bronze Age cannot be used for Palestine, which had its own development, even it if was influenced by Egypt. Or, the beginning of the Persian period (539 B.C.E.) cannot have had any effect on the material culture in Palestine and Syria before some time had elapsed.

Chronological Periods

Lower Paleolithic	ca. 1,5000,000—100,000 B.C.E.
Middle Paleolithic	100,000—40,000 B.C.E.
Upper Paleolithic	45/40,000—18,000 B.C.E.
Epipaleolithic	18,000—4500 B.C.E.
Kebaran	10,000—9000 B.C.E.
Natufian	9000—8500 B.C.E.
Prepottery Neolithic A (PPNA)	8500—7300 B.C.E.
Prepottery Neolithic B (PPNB)	7300—6000 B.C.E.
Pottery Neolithic	6000/5500—4500 B.C.E. [119]
Chalcolithic	4500—3500/3200 B.C.E.

Bronze Age	3500/3200–1200/1100 B.C.E.
Early Bronze I	3500/3200–3100 B.C.E.[120]
(Late EB I = Egyptian Dynasty 0)	
Early Bronze II (Dyn. I-III)	3100//2700/2650 B.C.E.
Early Bronze III (Dyn. IV-VI)	2700–2250 B.C.E.
Early Bronze IV (Intermediate period)	2250–2000/1950 B.C.E.[121]
Middle Bronze I[122] (Old MB IIA)	1950–1800 B.C.E.
Middle Bronze II (Old MB IIB-C)	1800–1550/1540 B.C.E.
Late Bronze I	1550–1400 B.C.E.
Late Bronze II	1400–1200/1100 B.C.E.[123]
Iron Age	1200/1100–539 B.C.E.
Iron I	1200–1000 B.C.E.
Iron II	1000-539 B.C.E.[124]
Persian Period	539–332 B.C.E.[125]

Abbreviations

ADAJ	Annual of the Department of Antiquities of Jordan
AncSoc	*Ancient Society*
ANET	*Ancient Near Eastern Texts Relating to the Old Testament,* 3rd ed., 1969
AnOr	Analecta Orientalia
ATANT	Abhandlungen zur Theologie des Alten und Neuen Testaments
BASOR	*Bulletin of the American Schools of Oriental Research*
Bib	*Biblica*
BN	*Biblische Notizen*
BO	*Bibliotheca orientalis*
BZAW	Beihefte zur ZAW
CBOT	Coniectanea biblica: Old Testament Series
CBQ	*Catholic Biblical Quarterly*
CRB	Cahiers de la Revue biblique
EncRel	*Encyclopedia of Religion*
FCBS	Fortress Classics in Biblical Studies
GBS	Guides to Biblical Scholarship
HTh	*History and Theory*

HTR	*Harvard Theological Review*
IDB	*Interpreter's Dictionary of the Bible,* 1962
JAOS	*Journal of the American Oriental Society*
JARCE	*Journal of the American Research Center in Egypt*
JBL	*Journal of Biblical Literature*
JCS	*Journal of Cuneiform Studies*
JNES	*Journal of Near Eastern Studies*
JR	*Journal of Religion*
JSOTSup	Journal for the Study of the Old Testament Supplement Series
JSS	*Journal of Semitic Studies*
KÄT	Kleine ägyptische Texte
MAOG	*Mitteilungen der altorientalischen Gesellschaft*
MDAIK	*Mitteilungen des deutschen archäologischen Instituts, Kairo*
Or	*Orientalia*
OT	Old Testament
OTL	Old Testament Library
OTS	*Oudtestamentische Studiën*
RivB	*Rivista biblica*
RM	Die Religionen der Menschheit
SAA	State Archives of Assyria

SAOC	Studies in Ancient Oriental Civilization
SBLMS	Society of Biblical Literature Monograph Series
SBT	Studies in Biblical Theology
SHANE	Studies in the History of the Ancient Near East
SSN	Studia semitica neerlandica
StudOr	*Studia Orientalia*
TCS	Texts from Cuneiform Sources
ThSt	Theologische Studien
TLZ	*Theologische Literaturzeitung*
VT	*Vetus Testamentum*
VTSup	VT Supplements
YNER	Yale Near Eastern Researches
ZA	*Zeitschrift für Assyriologie*
ZAW	*Zeitschrift für die alttestamentliche Wissenschaft*
ZRGG	*Zeitschrift für Religions- und Geistesgeschichte*

Notes

1. Hecataeus was one of the first Greek prose writers (late sixth century B.C.E.). For the quotation, see F. Jacoby, *Die Fragmente der griechischen Historiker,* vol. 1 (Leiden: Brill, 1957), 7. For Hecataeus, see, among others, L. Pearson, *Early Ionian Historians* (Oxford: Clarendon, 1939).

2. Emilio Gabba maintains that "before one attempts to evaluate critically the significance of any work or to use it for historical purposes, one must investigate the readership or audience for which it was intended, the aims of the author, and the means used to convey his thoughts and organize his text" ("Literature," *Sources for Ancient History,* ed. M. Crawford [Cambridge: Cambridge Univ. Press, 1983], 75).

3. "The whole truth at any stage of inquiry is an ideal that ought to be abolished from historiography, for it cannot ever be attained." D. H. Fischer, *Historians' Fallacies: Toward a Logic of Historical Thought* (New York: Harper & Row, 1970), 66.

4. R. Wittram illustrates this problem with the face of a person, which can be described if we

have some information about it, but its expressions and its voice are forever gone (*Das Interesse an der Geschichte* [Göttingen: Vandenhoeck & Ruprecht, 1958], 15–16).

5. For introductions to the theories of history and historiography, see, among others, E. H. Carr, *What is History?* (New York: St. Martin's, 1961); N. F. Cantor and R. I. Schneider, *How to Study History* (New York: Crowell, 1967); A. A. Moles, *Information Theory and Esthetic Perception,* trans. Joel F. Cohen (Urbana: Univ. of Illinois Press, 1966); B. Trigger, *Beyond History: The Methods of Prehistory* (New York: Holt, Reinhart, 1968); D. H. Fischer, *Historians' Fallacies: Toward a Logic of Historical Thought* (New York: Harper & Row, 1970); J. Deetz, *Man's Imprint from the Past: Readings in the Methods of Archaeology* (Boston: Little, Brown, 1971); M. I. Finley, *The Use and Abuse of History* (New York: Viking, 1975); *idem, Ancient History: Evidence and Models* (New York: Viking, 1986); E. Le Roy Ladurie, *The Mind and Method of the Historian,* trans. S. Reynolds and B. Reynolds (Chicago: Univ. of Chicago Press, 1987). See also G. H. von Wright, *Problems in the Theory of Knowledge* (The Hague: Nijhoff, 1972). Concerning Near Eastern historiography, see M. Liverani, "Memorandum on the Approach to Historiographic Texts," *Or* 42 (1973): 178–94; A. K. Grayson, "Histories and Historians of the An-

cient Near East: Assyria and Babylonia," *Or* 49 (1980): 140–94; J. Van Seters, *In Search of History: Historiography in the Ancient World and the Origins of Biblical History* (New Haven: Yale Univ. Press, 1983), 55–208. For history as a written medium for the elite, see, for instance, H. A. Hoffner, "Histories and Historians of the Ancient Near East," *Or* 49 (1980): 283–332. Concerning biblical historiography, see N. P. Lemche, "On the Problem of Studying Israelite History apropos Abraham Malamat's View of Historical Research," *BN* 23 (1984): 94–124. Compare also T. L. Thompson, *The Origin Tradition of Ancient Israel,* vol. 1, *The Literary Formation of Genesis and Exodus 1–23,* JSOTSup 55 (Sheffield: JSOT Press, 1987), esp. 22–25. As to the Hellenistic-Roman world, see A. Momigliano, *Alien Wisdom: The Limitations of Hellenization* (Cambridge: Cambridge Univ. Press, 1975); *idem, Studies in Historiography* (New York: Harper & Row, 1985); G. Shepers, "Some Aspects of Source Theory in Greek Historiography," *AncSoc* 6 (1975): 257–74.

6. See M. H. Gates, "Dialogues between Ancient Near Eastern Texts and the Archaeological Record: Test Cases from Bronze Age Syria," *BASOR* 270 (1988): 63–91.

7. Compare also the discussion in A. E. Glock, "Texts and Archaeology at Tell Ta'annek," *Berytus* 31 (1983): 57–66.

8. Consult M. R. Notis et al. in *Late Bronze and Early Iron Ages of Central Transjordan: The Baq'ah Valley Project, 1977-81,* ed. P. E. McGovern, University Museum Monographs 65 (Philadelphia: University Museum, Univ. of Pennsylvania, 1986), 272-78.

9. See G. W. Ahlström, "An Archaeological Picture of Iron Age Religions in Ancient Palestine," *StudOr* 55.3 (1984): 4-5.

10. Moles characterizes it as a "pseudo-language" in *Théorie des Objects* (Paris: Editions universitaires, 1972), quoted after C. A. Moberg, "Archaeology and Religion: What Do We Know?" *Temenos* 13 (1977): 98-99.

11. See the discussion by S. Piggot, *Ancient Europe from the Beginnings of Agriculture to Classical Antiquity* (Chicago: Aldine, 1966), 4-8.

12. Compare J. Deetz, *Invitation to Archaeology* (Garden City, N.Y.: Natural History Press, 1967), 1-7.

13. Compare Braudel, who divides history into three levels: "geographical time, social time, and individual time." The first level deals with "man in his relationship to the environment, a history in which all change is slow, a history of constant repetition." The second level is a "time with slow but perceptible rhythms," and the third level is that of "history of events" (*The Mediterranean and the Mediterranean World in the Age of Philip*

II, vol. 1, trans. S. Reynolds [New York: Harper & Row, 1972], 20-21).

14. This is the site where the Edomite royal city of Bozrah was located.

15. Braudel, *The Mediterranean,* 34.

16. See ibid., 278.

17. Compare Finley, who says that the ancients "found great voids in the inherited information about the past, or, worse still, quantities of data that included fiction and half-fiction jumbled with fact." The modern historian often tries to fill the void with source material based on oral tradition to a perhaps indeterminate extent (*Ancient History: Evidence and Models,* 16). In his book, *The Use and Abuse of History,* Finley also states that no historical documents existed in Greece before c. 700 B.C.E. (20). Tradition, he says, "did not merely transmit the past, it created it" (25).

18. I. Morris, *Burial and Ancient Society: The Rise of the Greek City-State,* New Studies in Archaeology (Cambridge: Cambridge Univ. Press, 1987), 24.

19. A. Momigliano, "Greek Historiography," *HTh* 17 (1978): 5. Compare J. A. Soggin, who states that the Mycenaean-Aegean world was "ignorant of writing" (*Introduction to the Old Testament: From its Origin to the Closing of the Alexandrian Canon,* OTL [Philadelphia: Westminster, 1976], 59).

20. As Momigliano points out, "Herodotus could be treated by turn as the father of history and as a liar, because nobody was in a position to check the stories he had told" ("Greek Historiography," 8).

21. "His is a kind of universal history; that is, it is the record of all the logical possibilities, political and human, that coexist in the human world," D. Grene, "Introduction," in *The History: Herodotus,* trans. D. Grene (Chicago: Univ. of Chicago Press, 1987), 21. We should note, for instance, that Herodotus had "at his disposal excellent information about the city of Babylon," according to P. Calmeyer, but the city "was described to him as the last capital of Assyria" ("Greek Historiography and Achaemenid Reliefs," in *Achaemenid History,* vol. 2, *The Greek Sources: Proceedings of the Groningen 1984 Achaemenid History Workshop,* ed. H. Sancisi-Weerdenburg and A. Kuhrt [Leiden: Brill, 1987], 20). This can be explained by the fact that in a Persian legend about the Three Empires, Assyria had replaced the neo-Babylonian empire (Calmeyer, *Greek Historiography,* 18–20).

22. In this connection we should note that Herodotus sometimes gives different accounts of one and the same event, as pointed out by J. Licht, "Biblical Historicism," in *History, Historiography*

and Interpretation, ed. H. Tadmor and M. Weinfeld (Jerusalem: Magnes, 1983), 107.

23. The term *saga* is in this presentation used in the modern sense. It should not be confused with the old Norse term, which could include both historiography and hagiography. A saga was often a chronicle dealing with the wars and feuds between particular clans describing their heroic courage and demands for justice. There were also some "fornaldar" (prehistoric) sagas. These mainly described adventures in which the heroes fought some "mythical" figures (trolls, monsters, and imaginary animals); see T. A. Anderson, *The Icelandic Family Saga* (Cambridge: Harvard Univ. Press, 1967).

24. I. Engnell, *Gamla Testamentet* (Stockholm: Svenska Kykrans Diakonistyrelses Bokforlag, 1945), vol. 1, 42–43; *idem, A Rigid Scrutiny: Critical Essays on the Old Testament,* trans. J. T. Willis (Nashville: Vanderbilt Univ. Press, 1969), 3–34. Compare also E. Nielsen, *Oral Tradition: A Modern Problem in Old Testament Introduction,* SBT 1/11 (Naperville, Ill.: Allenson, 1954); but see also his "The Traditio-Historical Study of the Pentateuch since 1945, with Special Emphasis on Scandinavia," in *The Productions of Time: Tradition History in Old Testament Scholarship,* ed. K. Jeppesen and B. Otzen (Sheffield: Almond, 1984), 16–19.

25. M. Noth, *A History of Pentateuchal Traditions,* trans. B. W. Anderson (Englewood Cliffs, N.J.: Prentice Hall, 1972), 1–2. Compare also S. Mowinckel, *The Spirit and the Word: Israelite Prophecy and Tradition,* ed. K. C. Hanson, FCBS (Minneapolis: Fortress Press, 2002; orig. ed. 1946); G. W. Ahlström, "Oral and Written Transmission: Some Comments," *HTR* 59 (1966): 69–70.

26. Concerning laws, Engnell also thought they were written down early (*A Rigid Scrutiny,* 66).

27. Ahlström, "Oral and Written Transmission," 73, 76–81.

28. The term *myth* is here used about texts in which god(s) or divine actions are mentioned, i.e., things that cannot be historically checked; see G. S. Kirk, *Myth: Its Meaning and Function in Ancient and Other Cultures* (Berkeley: Univ. of California Press, 1970). This is in contrast to P. Ricoeur, who sees myth as "a narrative of origins, taking place in a primordial time, a time other than that of everyday reality," in "Myth: Myth and History," in *EncRel* 10.273. This would mean that any saga, sacred or not, dealing with prehistoric periods is a myth.

29. For the role of myth in historiography, see G. Widengren, "Myth and History in Israelite-Jewish Thought," in *Culture in History: Essays in Honor of Paul Radin,* ed. S. Diamond (New York: Columbia Univ. Press, 1960), 467–95; J. Fränkel,

Dichtung und Wissenschaft (Heidelberg: Schneider, 1954); B. Albrektson, *History and the Gods,* CBOT 1 (Lund, Sweden: Gleerup, 1967); Finley, *Use and Abuse,* 11–33; J. J. M. Roberts, "Myth *versus* History: Relaying the Comparative Foundations," *CBQ* 38 (1976): 1–13; G. W. Ahlström, *Who Were the Israelites?* (Winona Lake, Ind.: Eisenbrauns, 1986), 45–55. See also E. W. Count, "Mythos as World View," in *Culture in History,* 580–627; W. G. Lambert, "Der Mythos im alten Mesopotamien, sein Werden und Vergehen," *ZRGG* 26 (1974): 1–16; J. Van Seters, *Der Jahwist als Historiker,* ThSt 134 (Zurich: Theologischer Verlag, 1987), 55–95.

30. S. Morenz, *Egyptian Religion,* trans. A. E. Keep (Ithaca, N.Y.: Cornell Univ. Press, 1973).

31. See Thompson, *Origin Tradition,* 78–79.

32. For the role of the sea, see H. G. May, "Some Cosmic Connotations of *Mayyim Rabbim,* Many Waters," *JBL* 74 (1955): 9–21; O. Kaiser, *Die mythische Bedeutung des Meeres in Ägypten, Ugarit und Israel,* BZAW 78 (Berlin: Töpelmann, 1959). Compare also B. F. Batto, "The Reed Sea: Requiescat in Pace," *JBL* 102 (1983): 27–35.

33. Crossing the river Jordan does not really require any miracle, because there are some passable fords.

34. Another famous invasion theory is the "Dorian invasion," which, according to A. M.

Snodgrass, among others, was not a migration from overseas, but more probably migrations within Greece (*The Dark Age of Greece: An Archaeological Survey of the Eleventh to the Eighth Centuries* [Edinburgh: Edinburgh Univ. Press, 1971], 311–13).

35. This is where N. K. Gottwald has misunderstood history, saying that "Israel *thought* it was different because it *was* different," in "Two Models for the Origin of Ancient Israel: Social Revolution or Frontier Development," in *The Quest for the Kingdom of God: Studies in Honor of George E. Mendenhall,* ed. H. B. Huffmon et al. (Winona Lake, Ind.: Eisenbrauns, 1983), 18. Gottwald has not shown as an empirical fact that Israel was different.

36. Van Seters sees the "conquest narrative" as a product of the D historian (*In Search of History,* 324). He also points out "how closely Dtr's work [the Deuteronomistic History] has been made to correspond with the literary pattern of military campaigns in the Assyrian royal inscriptions" (331).

37. G. Garbini emphasizes that there is "*no evidence* to provide a basis for the usual datings (those which can be found in textbooks); they are only chronological hypotheses" (*History and Ideology in Ancient Israel,* trans. J. Bowden [New York: Crossroad, 1988], xv).

38. Consult Momigliano, who states that the Hebrews showed no "distinction between a mythical age and an historical age" (*Essays in Ancient and Modern Historiography* [Middletown, Conn.: Wesleyan Univ. Press, 1977], 194).

39. See, for instance, R. O. Faulkner, "The Battle of Kadesh," *MDAIK* 16 (1958): 93–111.

40. See G. W. Ahlström, *Psalm 89* (Lund, Sweden: Gleerup, 1959), 57–104. E. Lipinski has seen David's relationship to Yahweh as that of a covenant between the god and his vassal. See *Le poème royale du Psaume LXXXIX 1-5, 20-38,* CRB 6 (Paris: Gabalda, 1967), 35–52. This is not to be denied, but the "Davidic covenant" is a late theological development with respect to the king's religious status.

41. J. Huizinga, "A Definition of the Concept of History," in *Philosophy and History: Essays Presented to Ernst Cassirer,* ed. R. Killansky and H. J. Paton (Oxford: Clarendon, 1936), 7–8; compare Van Seters, *In Search of History,* 1–2. O. Spengler states that "Classical history down to the Persian Wars, and for that matter the structure built up on traditions at much later periods, are the produce of an essentially mythological thinking" (*The Decline of the West,* vol. 1, *Form and Actuality,* trans. C. F. Atkinson [New York: Knopf, 1966], 10).

42. Consult M. Liverani, "Le 'origini' d'Israele—progetto irrealizzabile di recherché etnogenetica,"

RivB 28 (1980): 9–32.

43. The Akkadian term $^{mat}kaldu$ occurs no earlier than the first half of the ninth century B.C.E.; see H. W. F. Saggs, "Ur of the Chaldees: A Problem of Identification," *Iraq* 22 (1960): 200–207. For the Chaldeans, see J. A. Brinkman, "A Political History of Post-Kassite Babylonia 1158–722 B.C.E.," AnOr 43 (Rome: Pontifical Biblical Institute Press, 1968).

44. According to Van Seters, the phrase "Ur of the Chaldeans" (or "Ur *Kashdim*") "points directly to the Neo-Babylonian period" ("Confessional Reformulation in the Exilic Period," *VT* 22 [1972]: 454–55). Compare also W. M. Clark, "The Patriarchal Traditions. §2. The Biblical Traditions," in *Israelite and Judaean History,* ed. J. H. Hayes and J. M. Miller, OTL (Philadelphia: Westminster, 1977), 131.

45. See G. W. Ahlström, "Excursus: Abram/Abraham," in *The History of Ancient Palestine* (Minneapolis: Fortress Press, 1993), 180–87.

46. This is also emphasized by Noth, who has usually been criticized as having a low appreciation of the archaeological evidence. Noth maintains, however, that a history of the culture and politics of the ancient Near East must be built not only on the literary remains but also on a solidly built archaeological reconstruction (*Gebäude*).

Compare "Der Beitrag der Archäologie zur Geschichte Israels," in *Congress Volume: Oxford 1959,* ed. J. A. Emerton et al., VTSup 7 (Leiden: Brill, 1959), 264.

47. See J. A. Wilson in *ANET,* 25–29.

48. A. Malamat, "The Proto-History of Israel: A Study in Method," in *The Word of the Lord Shall Go Forth: Essays in Honor of David Noel Freedman in Celebration of His Sixtieth Birthday,* ed. C. L. Meyers and M. O'Connor (Winona Lake, Ind.: Eisenbrauns, 1983), 303–4.

49. Compare what Finley says about tribes: "No dogma is so pervasive about Greek history (or indeed Roman and 'Indo-European') as the one that there was a regular evolution from an early 'tribal' organization of society, based on kinship groups, to a political, territorial organization" (*Ancient History, Evidence and Models,* 90). See also C. H. J. de Geus, *The Tribes of Israel: An Investigation into Some of the Presuppositions of Martin Noth's Amphictyony Hypothesis,* SSN 18 (Assen: Van Gorcum, 1976), 130–50.

50. Thus de Geus, *The Tribes of Israel,* 130–31. See also N. P. Lemche, *Early Israel: Anthropological and Historical Studies on the Israelite Society before the Monarchy,* VTSup 37 (Leiden: Brill, 1985), 282–83.

51. Malamat, "The Proto-History of Israel," 305. The theory about a twelve-tribe amphictyony

(coalition), which supposedly constituted earliest Israel, has long been abandoned. The attempt to "resurrect" it in the form of a pan-Israelite league has not been successful. Nobody has been able to demonstrate the empirical fact of such a league. It is thus impossible to maintain, as does D. N. Freedmen, that the origin of the Pentateuch was some epic tradition of the twelfth century B.C.E. that had "its cultic locus in the amphictyonic festivals" ("Pentateuch," *IDB* 3.717). Compare also F. M. Cross, who sees "J and E as variant forms in prose of an older, largely poetic epic cycle of the era of the Judges" (*Canaanite Myth and Hebrew Epic* [Cambridge: Harvard Univ. Press, 1973], 293). For a critique of this theory, see S. Talmon, "The 'Comparative Method' in Biblical Interpretation—Principles and Problems," in *Congress Volume: Göttingen 1977,* ed. J. A. Emerton et al., VTSup 29 (Leiden: Brill, 1977), 352–56. Consult also C. Conroy, who states that *epic* ought to be abandoned "as a genre-term for the JE *Vorlage,*" "Hebrew Epic: Historical Notes and Critical Reflections," *Bib* 61 (1980):1–30.

52. Malamat's "method" is thus no method at all. For a critique of Malamat's theory, see N. P. Lemche, "On the Problem," 94–123. If Malamat's method were to be used for a reconstruction of the history of the United States of America, one

would have to write about almost all of the peoples of the world.

53. See also M. Roth's review of J. J. Finkelstein, "The Ox That Gored," *BO* 40 (1983): 399.

54. See Ahlström, *History,* chap. 7.

55. M. Liverani, "Political Lexicon and Political Ideologies in the Amarna Letters," *Berytus* 31 (1982):42.

56. Ibid., 44.

57. According to Josephus (*Apion* 1.112–125), the Annals of Tyre were translated into Greek and used by two Hellenistic historians, Menander of Ephesus and Dius. In these annals Solomon was supposedly mentioned. The reliability of this information may be disputed, but it is not impossible that certain records were kept in Tyre and other Phoenician cities. If so, Solomon could have been mentioned. As to the discussion, see H. Katzenstein, *The History of Tyre* (Jerusalem: Magnes, 1973), 77–80; Van Seters, *In Search of History,* 195–96; Garbini, *History and Ideology in Ancient Israel,* 23–24. B. Z. Wachholder believes that the historian Eupolemus (who could be the same as the one mentioned in 1 Macc 8:17) borrowed his knowledge about Solomon from Menander (*Eupolemus: A Study of Judeo-Greek Literature* [New York: Hebrew Union College–Jewish Institute of Religion, 1974], 110).

58. See W. Richter, *Exegese als Literaturwissenschaft; Einwurf einer alttestamentlichen Literaturmethode und Methodologie* (Göttingen: Vandenhoeck & Ruprecht, 1971). Richter's book is a good example of how necessary it is to differentiate between history and biblical historiography. For a review of his book, see J. W. Rogerson in *JSS* 20 (1975):117–22.

59. Tradition history, as advocated by Engnell (*Gamla Testamentet,* vol. 1), cannot be used because it refers to the prehistory of the text, something that we do not know anything about.

60. For the methods of form criticism and redaction criticism, see K. Koch, *The Growth of the Biblical Tradition: The Form-Critical Method,* trans. S. M. Cupitt (New York: Scribners, 1969); N. Habel, *Literary Criticism of the Old Testament,* GBS (Philadelphia: Fortress Press, 1971).

61. See T. E. Peet, *A Comparative Study of the Literatures of Egypt, Palestine and Mesopotamia* (London: Oxford Univ. Press, 1931); H. G. Güterbock, "Die historische Tradition und ihre literarische Gestaltung bei Babyloniern und Hethitern bis 1200," *ZA* 42 (1934):1–91 (15ff.).

62. Compare J. Barton, *Reading the Old Testament: Method in Biblical Study* (Philadelphia: Westminster, 1984), 52 (rev. ed. 1996).

63. Ehud was not a Benjaminite. The phrase *ben-hay^emînî* refers to a man from the "land of

Yemini" mentioned in 1 Sam 9:4. It was located in southern Ephraim just north of Bethel. This would mean that he was an Asherite.

64. See, for example, E. G. Kraeling, "Difficulties in the Story of Ehud," *JBL* 54 (1935): 205–10. C. Grottanelli sees the story as a literary parallel to Roman, Iranian, and Scandinavian narratives that, by means of military and/or cosmic symbolism, express victory over the forces of destruction ("Un passo del Libro dei Giudici alla luce della comparazione storico-religiosa: il guidici Ehud e il valore della mano sinistra," *Oriens Antiqui Collectio* 13 [1978]: 35–45).

65. See L. Alonso Schökel, "Erzählkunst im Buche der Richter," *Bib* 42 (1961):148–58. He also indicates that the narrator of the story knows that the time he has given to the story does not agree with reality (155).

66. His right hand was paralyzed: *'itter yah-y^{e}mînô* (v. 15). For the structure, see H. N. Rösel, "Zur Ehud Erzählung," *ZAW* 89 (1977): 270–72.

67. This shows that he was not a Benjaminite. Nothing is said about the participation of Benjamin and other Cisjordanian peoples in the war against Moab, neither is anything said about "the Israelites" of Transjordan as having joined Ehud.

68. The Latin translation and the LXX have read *ambidextrous*, "with restrained hand." Ehud

had made a sword, which is explained as a two-edged dirk a *gōmed* ("cubit") long. According to G. F. Moore, *gōmed*, which does not occur anywhere else in the Hebrew Bible, could be the same as Greek *pygmē*, "dirk" (*Judges*, ICC [Edinburgh: T. & T. Clark, 1895 repr. 1975], 94).

69. For the structure, see Richter, *Exegese*, 104–5.

70. See, for instance, the discussion by W. A. Ward and M. F. Martin, "The Balu'a Stele: A New Transcription with Paleological and Historical Notes," *ADAJ* 8-9 (1964): 5–29.

71. A literary unit has two (sometimes three) main actors. The others are only filling out the picture, like the crowd on a stage; see, for instance, Richter, *Exegese*, 96.

72. Compare Lemche, *Early Israel*, 383.

73. This means that the composition was made quite some time after Deborah's death. When she lived is not known.

74. Consult, for instance, J. Blenkinsopp, "Ballad Style and Psalm Style in the Song of Deborah: A Discussion," *Bib* 42 (1961): 61–76, esp. 64–65.

75. See, for instance, Peet, *Comparative Study*, 120–21; Güterbock, "Die historische Tradition," 15ff.; W. Helck, *Die Prophezeihung des Nfr.tj*, KÄT (Wiesbaden: Harrasowitz, 1970); H. Hunger and S. A. Kaufman, "A New Akkadian Prophecy Text," *JAOS* 95 (1975): 371–75; S. A. Kaufman, "Predic-

tion, Prophecy, and Apocalypse in the Light of New Akkadian Texts," in *Proceedings of the Sixth World Congress of Jewish Studies,* vol. 1 (Jerusalem: Hebrew Univ. Press, 1977), 221–28. See also R. D. Biggs, "The Babylonian Prophecies and the Astrological Tradition in Mesopotamia," *JCS* 37 (1985): 86–90.

76. Earlier I have maintained that there is a possibility of seeing the D history as having been written by one person (Ahlström, *Who Were the Israelites?* 76). This is also the understanding of H.-D. Hoffman, who sees the D historian as a composer using the pattern of change in presenting his religious history in which the sometimes fictional cult reforms play a large role (*Reform und Reformen: Untersuchungen zu einen Grundthema der deuteronomistischen Geschichtsschreibung,* ATANT 66 [Zurich: Theologischer Verlag, 1980]). This does not mean that the D historian did not use any literary sources. An indication that he used some written sources is the different spellings of some names; consult P. Machinist, "Assyria and its Image in First Isaiah," *JAOS* 103 (1983): 729.

77. The kings of the northern kingdom, Israel, are all denounced as being "evil," because in the narrator's view Israel was an apostate kingdom. From this point of view no Israelite king could have done what was "right in the eyes of Yahweh."

78. See Ahlström, *Who Were the Israelites?* 75–76. See also J. Wellhausen, *Die Composition des Hexateuchs und der historischen Bücher der Alten Testaments,* 3rd ed. (Berlin: de Gruyter, 1899; repr. 1963), 210–22.

79. A. K. Grayson, *Assyrian and Babylonian Chronicles,* TCS 5 (Locust Valley, N.Y.: Augustin, 1975), 43–45, 145–51; and *idem,* "Histories and Historians," 180. Grayson dates it to the latter part of the second millennium B.C.E. (*Assyrian and Babylonian Chronicles,* 278–79).

80. See G. W. Ahlström, *Royal Administration and National Religion in Ancient Palestine,* SHANE 1 (Leiden: Brill, 1982), 75–81.

81. Among the more recent publications dealing with this problem is that of J. M. Miller, who has not made the distinction between religious historiography and empirical history; see his "The Israelite Occupation of Canaan," in *Israelite and Judaean History,* ed. J. H. Hayes and J. M. Miller; Philadelphia: Westminster, 1977), 213. The same can be said about B. Halpern, *The Emergence of Israel in Canaan,* SBLMS 29 (Chico, Calif.: Scholars, 1983). In his most recent history, Miller is more cautious and says that "the main story line of Genesis–Joshua" is to be understood as an "artificial and theologically influenced literary product" (J. M. Miller and J. H. Hayes, *A History of*

Ancient Israel and Judah [Philadelphia: Westminster, 1986], 78).

82. See C. Redmount, "On an Egyptian/Asiatic Frontier: An Archaeological History of the Wadi Tumilat" (Ph.D. diss., University of Chicago, 1988). For a postexilic dating of these texts, see M. Bietak, "Comments on the 'Exodus,'" in *Egypt, Israel, Sinai: Archaeological and Historical Relationships in the Biblical Period,* ed. A. F. Rainey (Tel Aviv: Tel Aviv University, 1987), 163–71; D. B. Redford, "An Egyptological Perspective on the Exodus Narrative," in *Egypt, Israel, Sinai,* 137–61.

83. Redford, "An Egyptological Perspective," 138.

84. For this text, see G. W. Ahlström and D. Edelman, "Merneptah's Israel," *JNES* 44 (1985): 59–61; Ahlström, *Who Were the Israelites?* 37–42; F. Yurco, "Merneptah's Canaanite Campaign," *JARCE* 23 (1986): 189–215.

85. See J. Simons, *Handbook for the Study of Egyptian Topographical Lists Relating to Western Asia* (Leiden: Brill, 1937), 89–101, 178–86; W. Helck, *Die Beziehungen Ägyptens zu Vorderasien im 3. und 2. Jahrtausend v. Chr.,* 2nd ed., Ägyptologische Abhandlungen 5 (Wiesbaden: Harrasowitz, 1971), 167–69.

86. Compare Lemche, *Early Israel,* 414–15. See also T. L. Thompson, *Early History of the Israelite*

People: From the Written and Archaeological Sources, SHANE 4 (Leiden: Brill, 1993).

87. See, for instance, J. Wellhausen, *Prolegomena to the History of Israel* (New York: Meridian, 1957), 9. It is interesting to note that P, according to Wellhausen, presents the whole of Canaan "as a *tabula rasa*." The tribes then receive their inheritance by lot (358).

88. See the criticism by J. Pedersen, "Die Auffassung vom Alten Testament," *ZAW* 49 (1931):161–81. For a convenient résumé of this problem, see R. N. Whybray, *The Making of the Pentateuch: A Methodological Study,* JSOTSup 53 (Sheffield: JSOT Press, 1987), 17–131.

89. This would mean that the final composition of the Pentateuch is late. It is probably from the time after Ezra. Compare the discussion in R. Rendtorff, *The Problem of the Process of Transmission in the Pentateuch,* JSOTSup 89 (Sheffield: JSOT Press, 1990).

90. Compare Hoffner, "Histories and Historians," 283–332.

91. In a relief from Nineveh, Assyrian scribes are shown recording the captured people and the loot; see S. Parpola, *The Correspondence of Sargon II,* vol. 1, *Letters from Assyria and the West,* SAA 1 (Helsinki: Helsinki Univ. Press, 1987), 137.

92. P. Michaelowski, "Charisma and Control: On Continuity and Change in Early Mesopo-

tamian Bureaucratic Systems," in *The Organization of Power: Aspects of Bureaucracy in the Ancient Near East,* ed. M. Gibson and R. D. Biggs,
SAOC 46 (Chicago: Oriental Institute of the Univ.
of Chicago, 1987), 63.

93. K. A. Kitchen, *Pharaoh Triumphant: The
Life and Times of Ramesses II* (Warminster: Aris &
Phillips, 1982), 136–38.

94. See K. Bittel, *Hattusha: The Capital of the
Hittites* (New York: Oxford Univ. Press, 1970),
22–23.

95. A. J. Spalinger, *Aspects of the Military
Documents of the Ancient Egyptians,* YNER 9
(New Haven: Yale Univ. Press, 1982), 239.

96. Ibid., 118.

97. Grayson, *Assyrian and Babylonian Chronicles,* 11.

98. See Van Seters, *In Search of History,* 79–92.

99. For the settlement of different groups in the
central hills, see Ahlström, *Who Were the Israelites?* 12–36. Here we ought to remember that
Palestine had never had a homogenous population.
Also, the term *Canaanite* is not an ethnic term.

100. The letter J stands for the Yahwist, since in
the Germanic languages the first letter in the
tetragrammaton JHWH is an elongation of the
Latin I when used as a consonant. It is used also
in English Bibles when the tetragrammaton is
translated as Jehovah.

101. L. Rost dates the J work to the period of Solomon; "Sinaibund und Davidsbund," *TLZ* 72 (1947): 132. H. H. Schmid, on the other hand, maintains that the theology of the Yahwist is to be seen as a result of the problems of the fall of Judah and the Exile; *Der sogenannte Jahwist* (Zurich: Theologischer Verlag, 1976), 181.

102. Archaeologically, the Judean mountains were almost devoid of population before c. 1000 B.C.E.

103. The term *forced* can be defended from the point of view that when David had nullified the Saulidic dynasty the Israelites had no other choice than to accept David as their king.

104. See Ahlström, *Who Were the Israelites?* 103–4.

105. Momigliano, *Essays,* 141–42.

106. Of interest is that we do not even have an epic in the Hebrew Bible, as mentioned above.

107. Compare J. Barr, "Story and History in Biblical Theology," *JR* 56 (1976):5.

108. I. M. Diakonoff, "A Babylonian Political Pamphlet from about 700 B.C.E.," in *Studies in Honor of Benno Landsberger on his Seventy-Fifth Birthday,* ed. H. G. Güterbock and T. Jacobsen, Assyriological Studies 16 (Chicago: Univ. of Chicago Press, 1965), 343. For this text, which uses the style of omens in warning the king, see F.

M. T. Böhl, "Die babylonische Fürstenspiegel,"
MAOG 11.3 (1937):1–51.

109. These numbers, however, seem sometimes
to have been exaggerated.

110. It is, of course, impossible to find out how
much of this chronicle goes back to the "scribe"
(*sōpēr*) of the Solomonic court mentioned in 1 Kgs
11:41; nor do we know whether all the deeds of
Solomon were included in this chronicle; see also
Van Seters, *In Search of History,* 301–2.

111. These chronicles may originally have been
collections by royal scribes.

112. See Van Seters, *In Search of History,*
301–2.

113. See the material in Albrektson, *History
and the Gods;* Hoffner, "Histories and Historians,"
327–28; W. G. Lambert's criticism of Albrektson's
thesis misses the point, because Lambert brings
into the discussion the notion of monotheism as a
distinction between Mesopotamia and Israel as
far as ideas about the divine were concerned
("Destiny and Divine Intervention in Babylon and
Israel," *OTS* 17 [1972] 65–72). The phenomenon
of monotheism, however, is not a historical fact
in the Israel and Judah of the pre-exilic period. It
is a literary creation imposed on the past by the
Hebrew Bible, to urge the point of view of the
writers.

114. Around 1960 a German student asked me what philosophy I used in studying the history and religion of the Hebrew Bible. My answer was: "None. If I have a philosophy, it is that one cannot use any philosophical system." After that our ways parted.

115. A theological conception of history is exemplified by a statement of R. de Vaux: "Ultimately, however, human will and caprice have to give way to the demands of nature, which God himself uses to carry out his plans," *The Early History of Israel,* trans. D Smith (Philadelphia: Westminster, 1978), 3. A philosopher of religion may come to such a conclusion after having investigated a people's religious literature, but a historian can never demonstrate how any divine plan is carried out, simply because one cannot empirically demonstrate what any divine plan looks like.

116. The presentation in *The History of Ancient Palestine* therefore includes many statements about what could possibly have happened. I have sometimes been criticized for using too many "coulds," which I would rather do than stating some uncertainty as a fact. The historian's method is that of a detective. Because not all the facts are known, we have to use logic and draw conclusions

from what is known and from what (therefore) is or "could" be possible.

117. The pluvial periods are: the Lower Pleistocene (c. 600,000–300,000 B.C.E.), the Middle Pleistocene (c. 300,000–50,000 B.C.E.) and the Upper Pleistocene (c. 50,000–30,000 B.C.E.); see the résumé by A. Anati, *Palestine before the Hebrews* (New York: Knopf, 1963), 59–61.

118. For the reports, see L. Picard and U. Baida, *Geological Report on the Lower Pleistocene Deposits of the 'Ubeidiya Excavations* (Jerusalem: Israel Academy of Sciences and Humanities, 1966); M. Stekelis, *Archaeological Excavations at 'Ubeidiya, 1960–1963* (Jerusalem: Israel Academy of Sciences and Humanities, 1966); P. V. Tobias, *A Member of the Genus* Homo *from 'Ubeidiya* (Jerusalem: Israel Academy of Sciences and Humanities, 1966).

119. The period 6000–3750 B.C.E. is called "Developed Neolithic" by A. M. T. Moore, in "The First Farmers in the Levant," in *The Hilly Flanks and Beyond: Essays on the Prehistory of Southwestern Asia Presented to Robert J. Braidwood,* SAOC 36 (Chicago: Oriental Institute of the Univ. of Chicago, 1983), 11–42. For the Neolithic and Early Bronze Ages, see also L. E. Stager, "The Periodization of Palestine from Neolithic through

Early Bronze Times," *Chronologies in Old World Archaeology,* ed. R. Ehrich (Chicago: Univ. of Chicago Press, 1989), 85–114; compare H. Weippert, *Palästina in vorhellenistischer Zeit* (Munich: Beck, 1988), 27–32.

120. The beginning of EB I at Bab edh-Dhra' is dated to c. 3500 B.C.E. by G. R. Bentley, in "Kinship and Social Structure at Early Bronze IA Bab edh-Dhra', Jordan: A Bioarchaeological Analysis of the Mortuary and Dental Data" (Ph.D. diss., Univ. of Chicago, 1987, 80–87).

121. For the different suggestions about the terminology (Intermediate, EB-MB, or EB IV), and the dates, see Ahlström, *History,* chap. 3.

122. This terminology is also used by de Vaux, *Early History,* 833.

123. Because the use of iron was slow in coming, and because there is no real break in pottery tradition around 1200 B.C.E., one may see the Iron Age as starting at most places later than 1200 B.C.E.

124. The Neo-Babylonian period (c. 600–539 B.C.E.) could also be labeled Iron III.

125. This refers to the political dominions of the Persian empire. From the point of view of material culture, this period could as well be characterized as the Greco-Persian era.